LOOK UP TO SEE WHAT THE WEATHER WILL BE

BY GUY BROWN

in actual
eather Guy

ILLUSTRATED BY
MARIO LUGO

Science, Naturally!
An imprint of Platypus Media, LLC

D1417958

This book is dedicated to my father, Gary Stanley Brown. Thank you for nurturing me along the way, not only as a scientist, but as a person.

—Guy Brown

Guy's dad ♥

Look Up to See What the Weather Will Be
Hardback first edition • November 2021 • ISBN: 978-1-938492-42-6
Paperback first edition • November 2021 • ISBN: 978-1-938492-43-3
eBook first edition • November 2021 • ISBN: 978-1-938492-44-0

Written by Guy Brown, Text © 2021
Illustrated by Mario Lugo, Illustrations © 2021

Project Manager: Ellen E.M. Roberts, Bethlehem, PA
Senior Editor: Dia L. Michels, Washington, D.C.
Design and Doodle Art: Hannah Thelen, Silver Spring, MD
Cover Design: Caitlin Burnham, Washington, D.C.
Agent to the Illustrator: Patricia Padro, Queens, NY
Editorial Assistants:
    Amy Nash, Denver, CO
    Anna Tippett, Fredericksburg, VA
    Caroline Greaney, McLean, VA
    Destany Atkinson, Bowie, MD
    Emma Ferdinandi, Fresno, CA

Available in Spanish as Mira hacia arriba para ver cómo estará el clima
Paperback first edition • April 2022 • ISBN: 978-1-938492-73-0
eBook first edition • April 2022 • ISBN: 978-1-938492-74-7

Teacher's Guide available at the Educational Resources page of ScienceNaturally.com.

Published in the United States by:
    Science, Naturally!
        An imprint of Platypus Media, LLC
    725 8th Street, SE, Washington, D.C. 20003
    202-465-4798 • Fax: 202-558-2132
    Info@ScienceNaturally.com • ScienceNaturally.com

Distributed to the trade by:
    National Book Network (North America)
        301-459-3366 • Toll-free: 800-462-6420
        CustomerCare@NBNbooks.com • NBNbooks.com
    NBN international (worldwide)
        NBNi.Cservs@IngramContent.com • Distribution.NBNi.co.uk

Library of Congress Control Number: 2021939312

10 9 8 7 6 5 4 3 2 1

Printed in the United States

CONTENTS

 TEACHER'S GUIDE AVAILABLE

Hands-on activities, vocabulary, and additional resources are available in our Teacher's Guide. Download it today at the Educational Resources page of ScienceNaturally.com

INTRODUCTION

Every morning when it's still dark outside, I go to work to forecast the weather. I analyze data and reports to understand what is happening in the sky. My job is to let people know how to plan for their trip to work or school and how to prepare to go on a bike ride, visit grandma, or head to baseball practice.

If you walk outside and look up, you will probably see a cloud. Or two. Or twenty. I study the secrets they hold. Sure, clouds are just clusters of water droplets, but each day, I look again and again. I ask questions: What color? What size? How long has the cloud been around? Some clouds are so high, you need to be in an airplane to see them—some are so low, you can touch and taste them. Clouds tell us what is going on around and above us.

People are not the only ones who need to know what the clouds tell us about the approaching weather. Whether you are a parrot or a piranha, a python or a praying mantis, a porcupine or a person, your life depends on staying safe when bad weather strikes. I will show you how people and animals around the world respond to the clouds that cover us.

Guy Brown

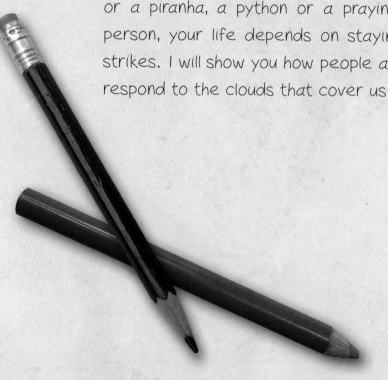

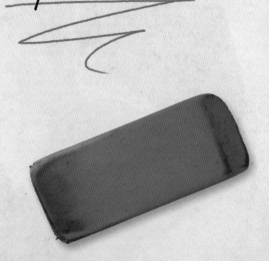

Chapter 1
THE HOW AND WHY OF STUDYING THE SKY

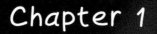

The sky is a busy place. For hundreds of years, people have been looking up to the sky to try and understand the world around them.

Stars can tell us the time of year, the sun can tell us the time of day, and the moon can tell us about the oceans' tides. Clouds can tell us many things, too, like if the weather will be calm or if a big storm is coming. There are people who devote their entire lives to studying the sky.

The word "meteor" comes from a Greek word meaning "things high up."
A person who studies the weather, like me, is called a
METEOROLOGIST.

I gather data collected from many different tools and, using
math and science, turn that data into a forecast. My job is to
communicate the weather forecast to my community.

TV STUDIO

In the United States and many parts of the world, anyone can gather scientific data. You can share your own weather observations with meteorologists to help keep them updated with local changes in the weather. Many citizen scientists, both children and adults, report their sightings with local meteorologists or national weather organizations.

I get to work before most people eat breakfast. I study the temperature, the speed and direction of the wind, the air pressure, and satellite images of clouds to determine what the weather will be. I can tell you when it's better to wear flip flops or rain boots.

I can forecast the weather many days in advance, which gives my community time to prepare for weather conditions. It's easier to stay safe if you know when to expect hail, strong winds, heavy rain, or fog.

My job is essential to the community. It is possible to predict the weather just by looking up at the sky, but the forecast is more accurate with the tools and technology used by meteorologists.

Chapter 2
WITH THESE TOOLS IN SIGHT, YOU CAN GET THE FORECAST RIGHT

There are two types of weather satellites.

POLAR ORBITING SATELLITES circle the Earth, gathering weather data. They can also monitor volcanic eruptions, forest fires, and ocean temperatures.

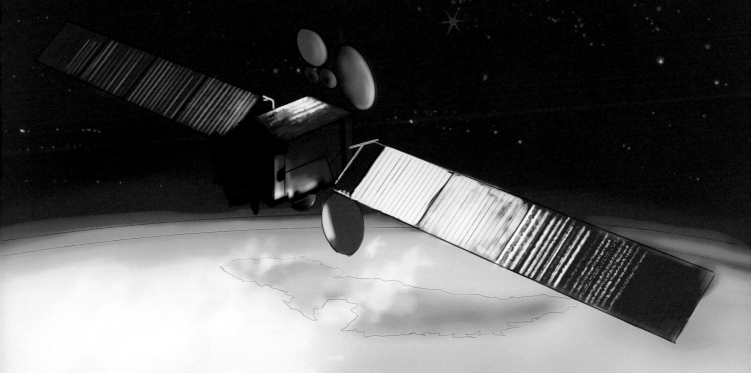

The other kind of satellite stays over one spot on the Earth. These GEOSTATIONARY SATELLITES let us know about cloud cover, lightning, and large storms such as hurricanes.

As technology improves, there could be new types of satellites to help weather forecasts become more accurate.

Satellites don't always show us the whole picture. Meteorologists need to keep track of many different measurements like temperature, air pressure, the oceans' tides, rainfall, and snow. With these tools, you can record your very own data:

RAIN GAUGE

Measures the amount of rain that has fallen.

RULER

Measures the amount of snow that has fallen.

TIDE STAFF

Measures the water level in the sea.

BAROMETER

Measures the weight, or pressure, of the air.

TV and radio meteorologists rely on a technology called Doppler Radar to understand which way raindrops are moving and how much precipitation is falling. This information helps them figure out the strength of a storm.

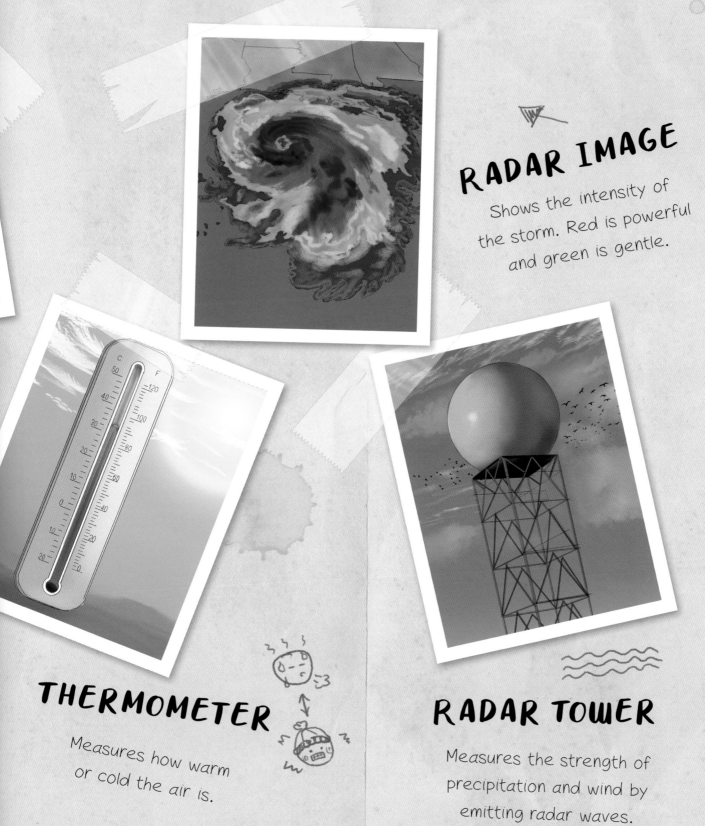

RADAR IMAGE

Shows the intensity of the storm. Red is powerful and green is gentle.

THERMOMETER

Measures how warm or cold the air is.

RADAR TOWER

Measures the strength of precipitation and wind by emitting radar waves.

WINDSOCKS are used to measure the speed and direction of wind. The windsock turns on its pole depending on the direction the air is moving. You can tell how strong the wind gusts are by how straight the cone is.

Windsocks are commonly used on airport runways where pilots can make note of the wind as they prepare for takeoff and landing.

When I go outside the studio to report on unusual or dangerous weather, it's called going "ON LOCATION."

My team travels in a special truck that is built to drive in bad weather and equipped with cameras and microphones. Reporting on location helps us get critical information and images to the community as quickly as possible.

Chapter 3
ANIMALS KNOW WHEN IT'S TIME TO GO

Tools and equipment help meteorologists like me give an accurate forecast, but you don't have to be on TV to make weather predictions. Animals sense changes in temperature, wind, humidity, and daylight.

Barn owls hunt at dusk and dawn, flying low over grasslands. Their very soft feathers are specially designed for silent flight, so they can hear and sneak up on small mammals scurrying on the ground. Barn owls are cautious of approaching rain or other conditions that can make it hard for them to fly.

Barn owls' delicate feathers are not waterproof—getting caught in a rainstorm would leave them waterlogged and stranded. Other birds don't have this issue. Some can produce waterproof oil; others take dust baths to protect their feathers. Barn owls don't have these ADAPTATIONS since dust or oil would make their silent wings too noisy.

Strong winds are dangerous, too. Barn owls weigh less than two pounds (one kg), so wind makes it hard for them to fly. They watch for signs of wet or windy weather, so they know when to seek safety.

Barns and hollow trees are warm, dry places that barn owls use to wait out bad weather. If they can't make it to shelter, they perch on a tree branch and try to stay dry under the leaves.

Like the barn owl, you know to seek cover in wet and windy weather. By heading indoors or carrying an umbrella when rain clouds roll in, you can stay safe and dry.

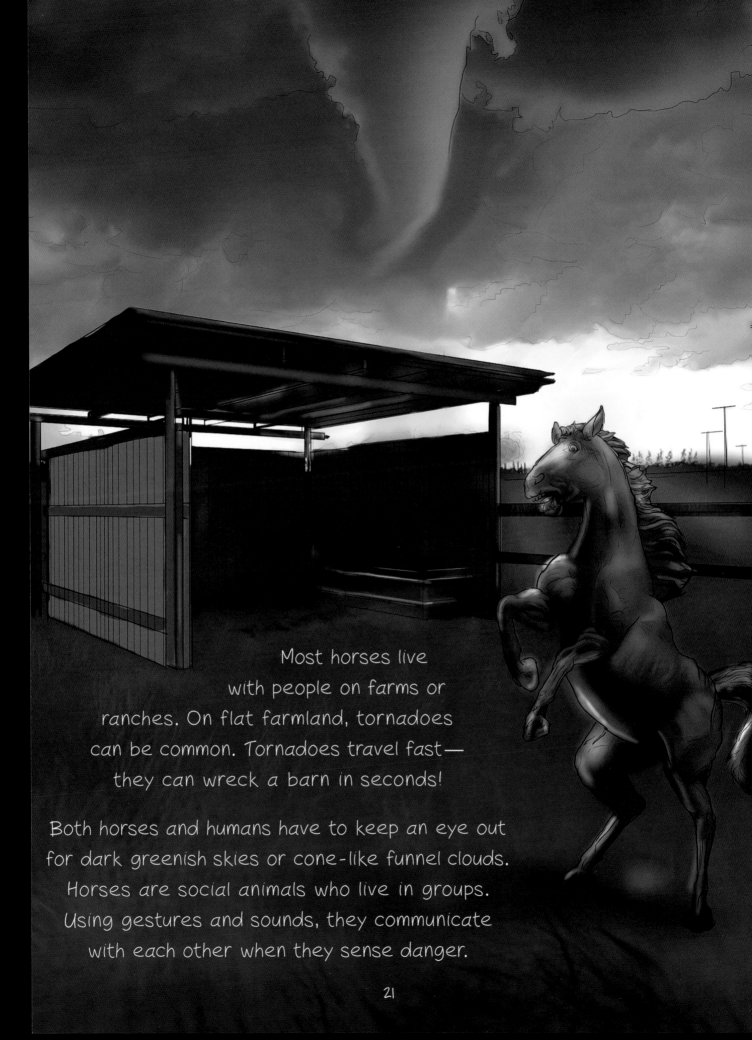

Most horses live
with people on farms or
ranches. On flat farmland, tornadoes
can be common. Tornadoes travel fast—
they can wreck a barn in seconds!

Both horses and humans have to keep an eye out
for dark greenish skies or cone-like funnel clouds.
Horses are social animals who live in groups.
Using gestures and sounds, they communicate
with each other when they sense danger.

Horses use their neighs and snorts as warnings, adding a rattling sound to their snort when they are extra scared. Humans and other animals can often tell when a storm is brewing by listening to horses.

Once the herd has been alerted to danger, horses run to find shelter. The average horse runs almost twice as fast as the average person. If it looks like a tornado is heading toward the barn, horse owners let the animals run free so they can stay out of the tornado's path. Horses can usually find their way back afterward, but some owners mark their horses so the animals can be returned home.

A tornado can leave quite a mess. Horse owners make sure their barns are
clear of broken branches, glass, and other objects tossed around by the storm.
The horses also need fresh water and food ready for when they return.

Like horses and their owners, you should take steps to keep yourself
safe. Listen to tornado warnings, move quickly to a secure place,
and have a weather safety kit to help you in the aftermath.

Food is hard to find during winter.
Grizzly bears survive by resting in a den for
several months. This is called HIBERNATION, and it
helps them save energy and stay safe and warm.

It's important for grizzly bears to be aware of signs of
changing weather so that they have time to prepare.
In the autumn, before hibernation, bears need to
eat a lot of food to store a thick layer of fat.

During this fall eating phase, called "HYPERPHAGIA," grizzly bears can eat 88 pounds (40 kg) of food in a day! To catch this much prey, bears rely on their keen sense of smell. They can sniff out another animal from over 18 miles (30 km) away.

The part of a bear's brain that controls their sense of smell is five times larger than a human's, and bears' noses have hundreds of tiny muscles. Bears are such good hunters that ravens trail behind them to eat their leftovers.

Grizzly bears build a winter den from a tree, a hole in the ground, or a cave. During hibernation, bears barely breathe, and their heartbeats slow down. They do not eat or drink, pee or poop. Their body uses the fat they stored up in the fall as food.

Just like bears, humans mostly stay inside in cold weather. While bears have extra layers of fat, we put on extra layers like coats, hats, boots, and gloves.

Chapter 4
ANIMALS AREN'T STRANGERS TO THE WEATHER'S BIG DANGERS

Most animals know how to escape weather dangers, but some animals have special adaptations to help them thrive in hazardous weather. On the coast, dense fog can make it impossible to see, but sea lions know how to overcome this challenge.

Sea lions live in colonies along the beach. They use their powerful flippers to catch fish and squid. In the summer, hundreds of sea lions raise their pups in a big group called a "ROOKERY." With frequent coastal fog, sea lions rely on their other senses to find food and to find each other.

Sea lions use their stiff, sensitive whiskers to feel where they are going and locate prey underwater. Mother sea lions spend many hours a day hunting, then return to the beach to nurse their pups. Even on foggy days, each mom must find her pup in the crowded, noisy rookery. Their great hearing helps moms pinpoint their pup's specific bark among hundreds of others.

Fog isn't the only challenge for sea lions. Sometimes the temperature gets too hot or too cold, but there's an adaptation for that, too.

Sea lions can regulate their temperature with a practice called "SAILING." They roll onto their sides and hold a flipper above the water. The position of the flipper allows them to cool down or warm up.

Humans cool themselves off by wearing fewer layers, finding shade, or by playing in the pool. In foggy weather, we don't have whiskers to help us, but we have other tools, like lighthouses. They help boats avoid crashing into the coast.

For a camel living in the desert, there is no escape from scorching temperatures. Some deserts are cloudless, with less than ten inches (25 cm) of rainfall per year. Without rain, water is hard to find.

Camels are really big, weighing up to one metric ton. They are herbivores, so they need to eat a lot of plants to survive. It's difficult for plants to grow without much water, but camels have adapted ways to get by.

Camels eat grasses, seeds, and grains when they can, but their leathery mouths can handle thorny twigs and leaves. It's a common myth that camels store water in their hump—it actually stores fat. In the same way that grizzly bears survive during hibernation, camels can live off of this stored fat for a long time.

Camels have adapted to desert sand, too. The sand is hot enough to cause burns, so thick pads, like cushions, protect their chests and knees when they lie down to sleep. Strong winds can also suddenly blow the sand into huge dust clouds, thousands of feet tall. This is called a sandstorm or HABOOB.

In a haboob, sand whips through the air. It is blinding and painful. Camels have three sets of eyelids and two rows of eyelashes to protect their eyes. They can even close their nostrils to keep from breathing in the sand.

People who live in or travel through the desert cover their skin with clothes to protect against sun and sand. In a haboob, they wear a hat over their eyes and tie a damp cloth around their mouth and nose.

Some animals have adaptations to help them take advantage of the weather. African elephants live in savannas, which are almost as dry as the desert. That's a problem for elephants, who drink up to 50 gallons (200 L) of water each day.

Elephants are the strongest land mammals, capable of uprooting trees. They use their powerful feet and tusks to dig for underground water, but it's easier to let the weather do the work!

With the largest ears of any animal, elephants can hear the sound of approaching storms. They listen for rain clouds being formed miles away. The herd heads to dry watering holes or stream beds near the storm, knowing the rain will fill them up.

Elephants don't seek cover in heavy rains. Their skin is thick, and they have a layer of fat that keeps them warm and dry. Elephants satisfy their thirst at the watering holes, but they also suck up water with their trunks and spray each other to cool down.

Adult elephants enjoy a good shower, but heavy rains can be dangerous to calves. Their skin is thin and tender. The calves stand underneath their mothers for protection.

When rain is in the forecast, humans also use it to their advantage. Some people put out rain barrels to collect drinking water or water for their gardens. You can try this too, but don't drink the rainwater unless it has been boiled to clean it.

Chapter 5
GUY WORKS ALL DAY, THEN IT'S TIME TO PLAY

Animals and humans alike are always responding to the weather. Every day I observe the world around me to assist with my weather forecasts. Just being curious and observant can get you started making your own daily forecast.

It took me years of practice collecting and studying information from satellites, radar, barometers, and other tools to understand how the smallest changes can affect the forecast. But the weather changes quickly. While I am outside, a simple glance at the clouds can tell me if a storm is brewing.

Look here

Don't forget that the animals you see every day are also reacting to the weather. Pay attention to how nearby animals are behaving, and use your senses just as they do. Use your ears like an elephant, your nose like a bear, and your eyes like a camel, and you'll be better prepared for approaching weather.

THE SKY IS THE LIMIT !!

Just like me, you can stay one step ahead of the changing skies.
Look up—and all around—to see what the weather will be!

 # MY WEATHER JOURNAL

By: _____

Doodle a cloud:

Doodle an animal:

After I saw this cloud,
the weather was:

_____

After I saw this animal,
the weather was:

_____

Notes: _____

_____

_____

_____

_____

_____

SUMMER SUN

Wear a hat, sunscreen, and sunglasses on bright days to protect yourself from the sun. Don't forget to stay hydrated.

THUNDERSTORM

BOOM!

Go inside as soon as possible and stay away from windows. Do not take a shower or bath. If you can't get inside, avoid water, crouch into a ball, and stay away from tall objects or anything made of metal.

SNOW

Bundle up with a coat, gloves, and hat before going outside, and wear sturdy boots to keep your feet warm. When it's icy, walk like a penguin!

FLASH FLOODS

Climb to the highest floor or other high ground during a flood. Don't walk or play near running water.

TORNADO

Get indoors and cover up with pillows, blankets, or a bike helmet. Go to the lowest floor possible and stay away from windows. A basement is the best option. If not, a bathroom, hallway, or closet will work.

DON'T BE SCARED! BE PREPARED!

Every family should have an emergency care kit in their home and car. The kit should have enough food and water for at least three days, warm clothes, a first aid kit, a flashlight, and a NOAA radio with batteries.

HURRICANE

Listen for evacuation orders. If directed, leave the area. Be prepared for power outages.

USING THE TABLE ON PAGE 49, CAN YOU GUESS WHAT EACH OF THESE CLOUDS MIGHT BE LIKE?

Here's an example. The name "stratocumulus" has two root words: "stratus" and "cumulus." Based on the table, stratocumulus clouds might be a flat sheet of puffy, blob-like clouds. Can you find them in the background of this page? How about the other clouds listed below?

Turn to the next page to see if you were right.

CIRRUS

STRATOCUMULUS

CIRROCUMULUS

NIMBOSTRATUS

CIRROSTRATUS

CUMULUS

ALTOCUMULUS

STRATUS

ALTOSTRATUS

CUMULONIMBUS

NOT ALL CLOUDS ARE THE SAME...
LEARN TO CALL THEM BY NAME

Clouds have names just like you and me! Clouds are given Latin names according to their height and shape in the sky. Each cloud can have a unique shape. Did you know the sun, mountains, and weather fronts can morph and shape the clouds you see in the sky?

Low clouds block sunlight and make the daytime cloudy and cool. The Earth receives more sun as clouds move higher in the sky. The wind can blow high clouds faster than 100 miles per hour (160 km/hr)!

ROOT WORD	ORIGINAL MEANING	HOW IT LOOKS
Cumulus	heap, pile	puffy, blob-like, in a group
Stratus	layer, sheet	flat, blanket-like
Cirrus	fiber, hair	wispy, strand-like
Nimbus	rain, precipitation	dark, thick, brings storms
Alto	high	high up but not the highest

HIGH CLOUDS
20,000 – 35,000 ft
(6,096 – 10,668 m)

CIRRUS

Appears when sunny, but could mean warmer or stormy weather coming soon.

CIRROCUMULUS

Enjoy the sun, but there could be a storm or hurricane on the way if you live next to the beach.

MIDDLE CLOUDS
6,500 – 20,000 ft
(1,981 – 6,096 m)

ALTOCUMULUS

Seen in the morning, this could mean thunderstorms in the evening.

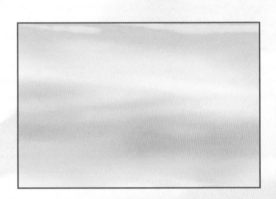

ALTOSTRATUS

Pack an umbrella! Continuous rain or snow could be on the way.

LOW CLOUDS
0 – 6,500 ft
(0 – 1,981 m)

STRATOCUMULUS

Rain or snow is rare. Usually means dry weather.

STRATUS

These clouds can touch the ground and make it foggy, cloudy, or drizzly.

CIRROSTRATUS

Appears one day before rain or snow.

What Are Clouds Made of?

High Clouds = ice crystals

Middle Clouds = ice crystals
+
water droplets

Low Clouds = water droplets

Towering Clouds = ice crystals on top
+
water on the bottom

TOWERING CLOUDS:

Cumulus and cumulonimbus clouds can start low in the sky and grow very tall into the higher levels of the sky.

CUMULONIMBUS

Big, dark, thunderstorm clouds that grow tall. A tornado could be possible.

NIMBOSTRATUS

It's currently raining or snowing out! These low clouds can sometimes rise to the middle level.

CUMULUS

Appears in many different shapes on a sunny day.

MY WEATHER WORDS

Atmosphere: layers of gases surrounding Earth, held in place by Earth's gravity.

Cloud: a large collection of very tiny droplets of water or ice crystals floating in the atmosphere.

Condensation: the process where water vapor (water in its gas form) cools and turns into liquid water.

Damp: a little wet; moistened.

Dawn: the time in the morning before sunrise when daylight first appears.

Doppler Radar: a weather radar that is used to track the rate and direction of precipitation and wind.

~~Drowt~~ ~~Drоht~~ ~~????~~ **Drought**: an extended period of dry weather that can lead to a water shortage and damaged crops. Droughts can last for months.

Dusk: the time in the evening after sunset when daylight transitions to night.

Ecosystem: all of the living and nonliving things in a specific area where the organisms work together as a unit.

Flood: rising water rushing over land; usually a result of heavy rain or the melting of several inches of snow, which causes rivers or lakes to overflow.

Fog: a cloud on the ground; mist or water droplets suspended in the air at Earth's surface, which can be hard to see through.

High Pressure System: cool, dry air that typically brings sunny skies and a light breeze.

Hurricane: a large and powerful storm in the Atlantic Ocean, Gulf of Mexico, or Caribbean Sea, with heavy rainfall and winds ranging between 74 miles per hour and 150 miles per hour (120 km/hr to 240 km/hr) or greater.

~~Lightxning~~ **Lightning**: a blazing hot electrical spark generated by thunderstorms; it can strike from cloud to cloud or cloud to ground, and it travels at the speed of light, which is approximately 671,000,000 miles per hour (1,080,000,000 km/hr).

Low Pressure System: warm, wet air that brings storms and strong winds.

NOAA (The National Oceanic and Atmospheric Administration): an American scientific agency that focuses on the conditions of the oceans, major waterways, and the atmosphere.

Overcast: when thick clouds cover at least 90% of the sky, causing it to look dull and gray.

~~Presi~~ **Precipitation:** any form of water from the atmosphere, such as rain, snow, sleet, ice pellets, and hail.

Snow: precipitation that is made of ice crystals. Snow can stick together to create snowflakes that fall from the sky.

Temperature: how hot or cold something is, measured with a thermometer and recorded on the Celsius (°C), Fahrenheit (°F), or Kelvin (K) scales.

Thunderstorm: a storm that usually means wind, lightning, thunder, dense clouds, heavy rain, or hail.

Tide: the constant rise and fall of Earth's oceans (and lakes, and even your cup of water, though it's very small) caused mainly by the gravitational pull of the Moon.

~~Tornadoe?~~ **Tornado:** an aggressive rotating column of air that extends from a thunderstorm to the ground. The winds can exceed 300 miles per hour (480 km/hr).

Water Cycle: the movement and changing states of water as it travels around Earth's oceans, atmosphere, and land. The states are liquid water, solid ice, and water vapor or gas.

Water Droplets: very small beads of water.

Waterlogged: soaked; full of water.

~~Wether~~ **Weather:** the state of the atmosphere regarding wind, temperature, moisture, cloudiness, and pressure, among other factors.

Weather Forecast: a description of what the weather is most likely to be in the near future.

Wind: the movement of large amounts of air in a specific direction.

Wind Gust: rapid wind speed changes.

ABOUT THE AUTHOR

GUY BROWN has been fascinated by the sky since the age of nine, when he decided he wanted to be an expert at forecasting the weather. He studied Electronic Media/Film and Meteorology at Towson University in Maryland. Guy made his debut as a TV meteorologist in Cheyenne, Wyoming and later worked for a local TV station in Madison, Wisconsin. You can find Guy forecasting the weather on-air today in the Minneapolis-St. Paul area of Minnesota. Guy enjoys volunteering at local elementary schools, where he shares his passion for meteorology with children. He also dabbles in acrylic painting and is an active member of the National Weather Association and the National Association of Black Journalists.

Email: GUY.BROWN@SCIENCENATURALLY.COM
Visit: WWW.YOURWEATHERGUY.COM

ABOUT THE ILLUSTRATOR

MARIO LUGO resides in Sao Paulo, Brazil. He was born in San German, Puerto Rico. Fluent in Portuguese, Spanish, and English, he loves to express himself through art. He has taken painting, drawing, and computer science classes, but is largely self-taught. With his twin brother, Manuel, Mario relocated to Sao Paulo in 2018, where he established himself as an illustrator and tattoo artist. *Look Up to See What the Weather Will Be* is his first book.

Email: MARIO.LUGO@SCIENCENATURALLY.COM